los

Please return/renew this item by the last date shown

HOW DOES
IT GROW?

BUTTERFLY

Jinny Johnson
Illustrations by Michael Woods

FRANKLIN WATTS
LONDON•SYDNEY

An Appleseed Editions book

First published in 2009 by Franklin Watts
338 Euston Road, London NW1 3BH

Franklin Watts Australia
Hachette Children's Books
Level 17/207 Kent St, Sydney, NSW 2000

Created by Appleseed Editions Ltd,
Well House, Friars Hill, Guestling,
East Sussex TN35 4ET

Designed by Helen James
Edited by Mary-Jane Wilkins
Picture research by Su Alexander

ISBN 978 0 7496 8788 5

Dewey Classification: 595.7'33

A CIP catalogue for this book is available from the British Library.

Photograph acknowledgements
page 9, 17 & 29 Patti Murray/Photolibrary Group;
19 Richard Shiell/Photolibrary Group
Front cover Richard Shiell/Photolibrary Group

Printed in China

Franklin Watts is a division of Hachette Children's Books,
an Hachette Livre UK company.
www.hachettelivre.co.uk

Contents

Tiny eggs

Who do you think **laid these eggs**? Each one is shaped like a **tiny barrel** and is only about as big as the **head of a pin**.

The eggs are resting on the leaf of a **thistle plant**. They are slightly **sticky** so they do not fall off the leaf.

The eggs were laid by a **painted lady butterfly** and they will hatch in about five days' time.

THE FEMALE BUTTERFLY LAYS LOTS OF EGGS ON DIFFERENT LEAVES.

What will hatch out of the eggs?

First days

A **caterpillar crawls** out of each egg. All **butterflies and moths** spend the first part of their lives as caterpillars.

The **painted lady** caterpillar is tiny when it first hatches – it could sit on your **little fingernail**. The caterpillar has **prickly hairs** all over it.

The caterpillar **begins to eat** straight away. It needs lots of food to help it **grow** and **turn into a butterfly**.

What does the caterpillar eat?

Hungry caterpillar

The caterpillar first eats its own **egg case**, then the leaf it hatched on. It **eats as much as it can**.

The caterpillar has **strong jaws** for **munching** leaves and **three pairs of legs** for moving around. It also has several pairs of **prolegs**. These look like **extra legs** and they help the caterpillar hold on to leaves and stems.

Thistles are a **favourite food**. The caterpillar also eats the leaves of **hollyhocks, mallows** and other plants.

A PAINTED LADY
CATERPILLAR ON
A THISTLE.

What happens when the caterpillar grows bigger?

New skin

As the caterpillar grows, its **skin** becomes **very tight** – just as your clothes feel **too small** for you **when you grow**.

When the caterpillar grows too big for its skin it **moults**. This means that the **old skin splits** and comes off. Underneath the caterpillar has grown **a new, larger skin**.

A caterpillar **moults** four or five times as it grows to its full size.

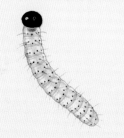

THE CATERPILLAR GROWS VERY QUICKLY.

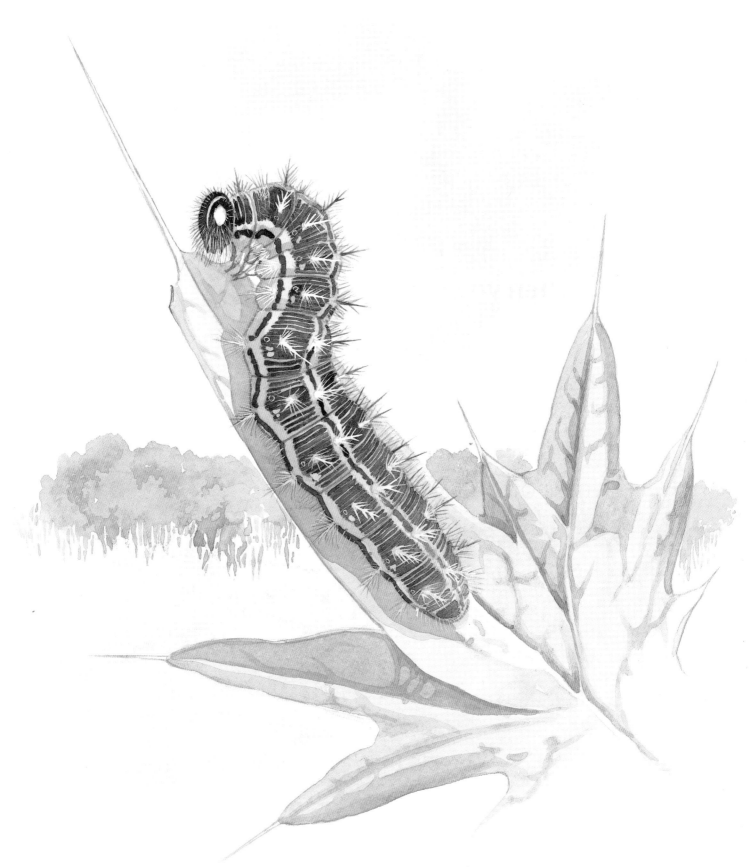

How big does the caterpillar grow?

The next stage

The **caterpillar grows** until
it is around 4 cm long – that's
about the size of your little finger.
Now it is time for the caterpillar
to **become a butterfly**.

It finds a safe place and **spins
a thread of silk**. It hangs on the
thread from a branch or twig
with its body in a curved shape.

Soon its **skin** will **split open**
and inside will be a **chrysalis**.

SOME WASPS CATCH
CATERPILLARS TO FEED
TO THEIR YOUNG.

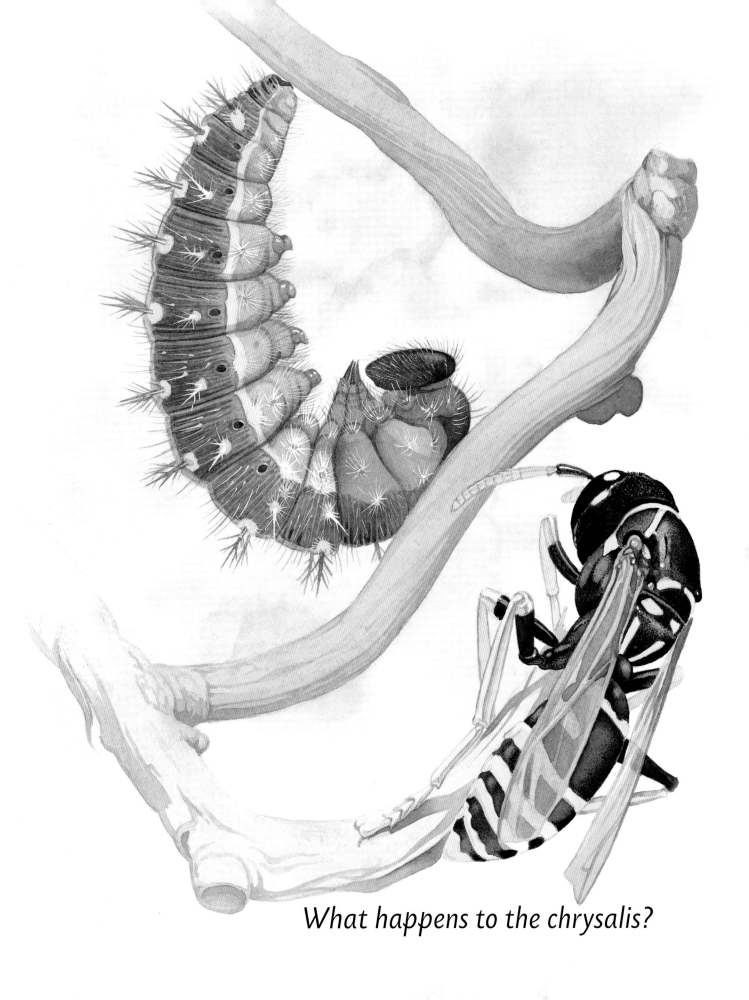

What happens to the chrysalis?

Big changes

A painted lady **chrysalis** is usually **brownish** with some **gold-coloured spots**. Amazing things happen inside the chrysalis during the next week or ten days.

The caterpillar's **body turns to liquid** – like caterpillar soup. Then it reshapes itself as a **butterfly** with **wings and legs**.

When the butterfly is almost ready, the **chrysalis** becomes **transparent**.

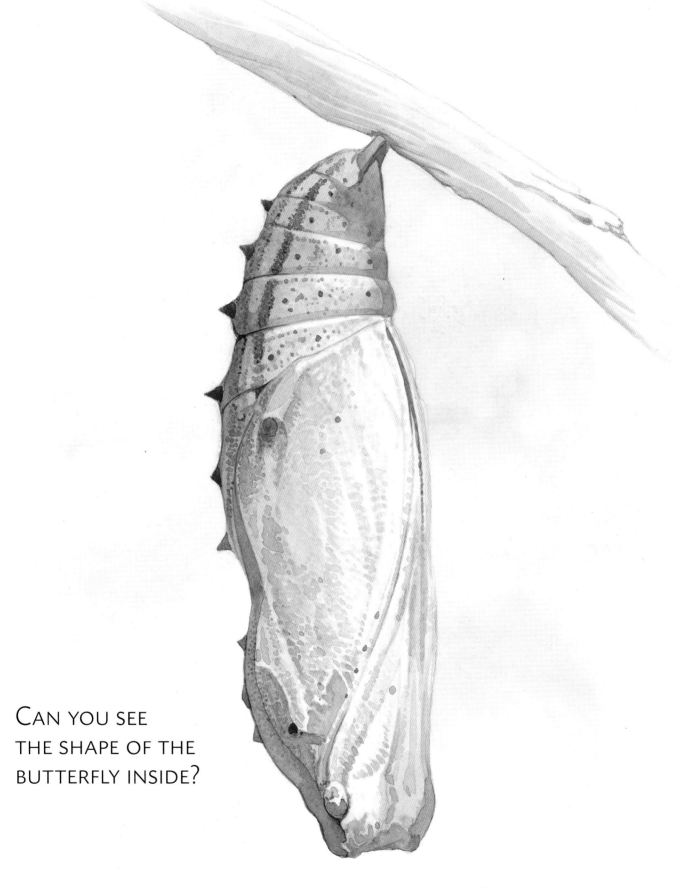

CAN YOU SEE
THE SHAPE OF THE
BUTTERFLY INSIDE?

How does the butterfly come out?

A butterfly!

The chrysalis **splits open** near the bottom and the butterfly's head **peeks out**. Then its **wings** and **legs** appear.

When the **butterfly** first comes out it **clings** to the **twig** for a while to recover. Its wings are crumpled. Slowly **blood flows** into the **wings** and they **spread out**.

The butterfly has to wait for its wings to **strengthen** and **dry** before it can **fly**.

THIS BUTTERFLY IS ALMOST OUT OF ITS CHRYSALIS.

When will the butterfly be able to fly?

Flying away

The **painted lady butterfly** is ready to fly away a few hours after it **comes out** of its chrysalis.

It has **two pairs of wings**, as all butterflies do, and it **flaps** both pairs together as it flies.

The wings are covered with **tiny** overlapping **scales**. These scales make the **beautiful patterns** and **colours** on a butterfly's wings.

Do male and female painted ladies look the same?

Beautiful wings

Male and female painted ladies look almost the same, but their markings are **slightly different**.

The **markings** on the **top** of their **wings** are different from the markings **underneath**.

Painted lady butterflies like to fly in open **fields** and **meadows** where there are plenty of **flowers**. Butterflies help flowers grow by **carrying pollen** from one flower to another as they **feed**.

THE MALE BUTTERFLY (TOP) SHOWS OFF HIS BRIGHT MARKINGS TO THE FEMALE.

What do butterflies eat?

Food from flowers

Adult painted ladies aren't as greedy as caterpillars. They feed **only** on a **sweet liquid** from flowers called **nectar**.

The butterfly has a **long mouth** shaped like a tube or a drinking straw. It **sucks up** the **nectar** with this. When the butterfly isn't eating, it keeps the **feeding tube** curled up out of the way.

A BUTTERFLY SUCKS UP SWEET NECTAR.

How does the butterfly find food?

Butterfly senses

A butterfly's **sense of smell** helps it to find sweet **flower nectar** to eat. Its **antennae** pick up smells and it can also smell with its feet!

A **male** butterfly's antennae also help it to find **a female mate** by smell.

A butterfly has **big eyes**, too, and sees the world in **colour**.

LOOK AT THIS BUTTERFLY'S LONG ANTENNAE.

How long do butterflies live?

Starting again

Most **butterflies** don't live very long after they have **changed** from **caterpillars** into adults.

The **painted lady** lives only two or three weeks. It has just enough time to **find a mate** and **lay eggs**.

The female lays her eggs on **plant leaves**. She may lay as many as **500 eggs** in her lifetime. Soon new caterpillars will **hatch** and start to eat!

CAN YOU SEE THE TINY EGGS THIS BUTTERFLY HAS LAID?

More about butterflies

Where do butterflies live?

Butterflies live all over the world, except in the coldest places. The painted lady is just one of thousands of different kinds of butterfly. It lives in North and South America, Asia, Europe and Africa. All butterflies are insects.

The life cycle of a butterfly

Like all butterflies and moths, the painted lady spends the first part of its life as a caterpillar. The caterpillar's purpose in life is to grow big and strong enough to turn into a butterfly. The transformation of the caterpillar into a butterfly is called metamorphosis. The butterfly's job is to fly away, find a mate and produce more eggs.

What do butterflies do?

Butterflies are important because they pollinate plants. As they gather nectar from flowers, pollen grains stick to their bodies. The butterflies then carry the pollen to the next flower they visit.

A PAINTED LADY BUTTERFLY
TAKING NECTAR FROM A FLOWER.

Words to remember

antennae

A pair of long thin parts on a butterfly's head that help it sense things around it.

caterpillar

The young of a butterfly which has a different body shape from the adult.

chrysalis

The stage in a butterfly's life when it is changing from a caterpillar to a butterfly.

feeding tube

A butterfly's long tube-like mouth, like a drinking straw.

moults

To shed an old skin, revealing a new one underneath.

nectar

A sugary liquid in flowers.

pollen

Tiny powdery grains made by flowers.

pollinate

The way pollen reaches a plant's eggs so it can make seeds.

silk

Strong thread spun from the caterpillar's body.

Websites

Children's Butterfly Site
http://www.kidsbutterfly.org/

Earth's Birthday Project
www.earthsbirthday.org/butterflies/bflys/activitykit/2.html

Enchanted Learning
www.enchantedlearning.com/subjects/butterfly/activities/
printouts/paintedlady.shtml

Index